THE SECOND Garfield TREASURY

THE SECOND
Garfield
TREASURY

JIM DAVIS

GARFIELD: © 1978 United Feature Syndicate, Inc.

BALLANTINE BOOKS • NEW YORK

The Sunday strips appearing here in color were previously included in black and white in GARFIELD Weighs In, GARFIELD Takes the Cake, GARFIELD Eats His Heart Out, and GARFIELD Sits Around the House.

Library of Congress Catalog Card Number: 83-90071

ISBN 0-345-33276-8

Manufactured in the United States of America

Designed by Gene Siegel

First Edition: November 1983

10   9   8   7   6   5   4   3

This book is dedicated to the cartoonists whose strips were in the Marion Chronicle-Tribune, Marion, Indiana, in the early '50s. They were the ones who inspired me to become a cartoonist and influenced my philosophy of cartooning.

This book is dedicated to: Sparky Schulz (Peanuts), who proved there is humor in the gentle things in life; Milton Caniff (Steve Canyon), who whisked me away to exotic places I never dreamed existed; Mort Walker (Beetle Bailey), whose every line and every word was distilled into pure humor; Hal Foster and John Cullen Murphy (Prince Valiant), who set an artistic standard that will never be matched again; Chic Young (Blondie), who taught me the value of interpersonal relationships in a strip; and Walt Kelly (Pogo), who carved a niche on the comics page for true creative genius.

This book is dedicated to my mentors...my friends.

JIM DAVIS

SLOSH!

JIM DAVIS

GABING!

8-10

© 1980 United Feature Syndicate, Inc.

8-24

DID YOU EVER OWN A CAT, LYMAN?

I GREW UP WITH FOUR OF 'EM

WHAT WERE THEIR NAMES?

LET'S SEE...

THERE WAS "CAT," "CAT," "CAT" AND "CAT"

NO NAMES?

WHAT'S THE USE OF NAMING A PET THAT WON'T COME WHEN YOU CALL IT?

GOOD POINT

JIM DAVIS

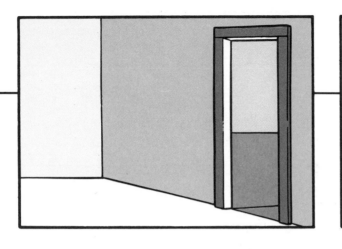

© 1980 United Feature Syndicate, Inc.

9-14

JiM DAViS

JIM DAVIS

THIS CHAIR COULD USE SOME SOFTENING UP

BOING BOING BOING

9-28

SCRATCH SCRATCH SCRATCH

MUCH BETTER

© 1980 United Feature Syndicate, Inc.

SPROING

JUST WHEN A CHAIR EARNS YOUR RESPECT, IT TURNS ON YOU

© 1980 United Feature Syndicate, Inc.

10-5

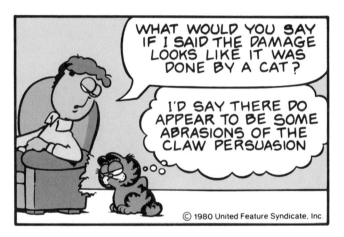

11-9

WHOCK!

SPLAT!

JIM DAVIS

© 1980 United Feature Syndicate, Inc.

JIM DAVIS

11-23

HELLO? FUNNY FARM? DO YOU TAKE PETS?

© 1980 United Feature Syndicate, Inc.

JIM DAVIS   12-21

NO SWEAT, SARGE. I'LL TAKE THAT MACHINE GUN NEST OUT WITH MY TRUSTY BAZOOKA HERE

SO THIS IS WHAT IT FEELS LIKE TO BE POTATO SALAD

12-28

RHETT, RHETT. WHATEVER SHALL I DO? WHEREVER SHALL I GO?

TAKE ME TO YOUR LEADER, EARTHLING, OR I'LL ATOMIZE YOUR FACE

© 1980 United Feature Syndicate, Inc.

THAT FOOD'S FOR EATING, GARFIELD

WHAT ARE YOU TRYING TO DO? MAKE ME SICK OR SOMETHING?

JIM DAVIS

WHY, HELLO THERE

I'M LOST

AREN'T YOU CUTE!

CAN YOU GIVE ME DIRECTIONS?

2-1

RUN ALONG NOW, KITTY

WHAT DID I DO?

JIM DAVIS

JIM DAVIS

2-8

AREN'T PET STORES FASCINATING, GARFIELD?

THE CUTE HAMSTERS, THE CANARIES, THE TROPICAL FISH

4-12

GARFIELD?

GARFIELD?!!

OH, THERE YOU ARE

COME ON. LET'S GO HOME FOR LUNCH

NO THANKS. I JUST ATE

JIM DAVIS

© 1981 United Feature Syndicate, Inc.

CLOBBER

© 1980 United Feature Syndicate, Inc.

JIM DAVIS   5-10

© 1981 United Feature Syndicate, Inc.

GOING TO DO SOME SINGING ON THE OL' FENCE TONIGHT?

MUSIC IS MY LIFE

7-26

JIM DAVIS

© 1981 United Feature Syndicate, Inc.

© 1981 United Feature Syndicate, Inc.

YOU KNOW, SOME FOODS ARE FUNNIER THAN OTHERS

10-18 JIM DAVIS

BEETS ARE FUNNY

LIVER... NOT FUNNY

PRUNES ARE FUNNY, POTATOES AREN'T

CHICKEN, NOW THAT'S FUNNY

© 1981 United Feature Syndicate, Inc

HOW ABOUT PICKLES AND KUMQUATS FOR LUNCH, GARFIELD?

WAH HA HA!

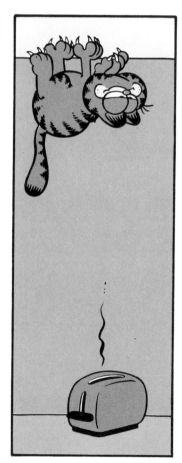
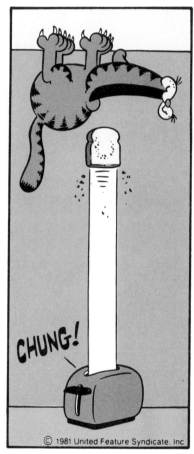

CHUNG!

GARFIELD WILL BE IN HERE ANY MINUTE TO WAKE ME FOR BREAKFAST

11-8 JIM DAVIS

HE'LL PRY MY EYE OPEN TO SEE IF I'M AWAKE

© 1981 United Feature Syndicate, Inc.

THEN HE WILL TAP DANCE ON MY HEAD

AND THEN HE'LL SIT ON MY CHEST AND BREATHE IN MY FACE UNTIL I GET UP!

OKAY! OKAY!

WHAT DID I DO?

© 1981 United Feature Syndicate, Inc.

© 1981 United Feature Syndicate. Inc.

JiM DAViS

11-22

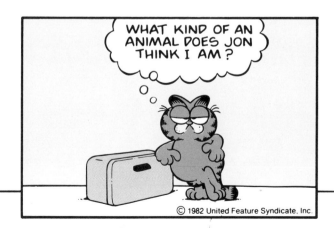

LAST ONE IN'S A ROTTEN EGG!

YOU FIRST, POOKY

BACK FLIP!

© 1982 United Feature Syndicate, Inc.

3-21

JIM DAVIS

CHOMP!
SLURP! GULP!

Z

STAY OUT OF
MY DREAMS

© 1982 United Feature Syndicate, Inc.

JIM DAVIS

3-28

4-4

JIM DAVIS

5-16

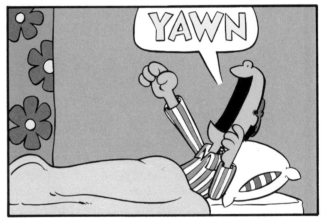

© 1982 United Feature Syndicate, Inc.

JIM DAVIS

7-4

TOUCH MY FOOD AND
YOU'RE ONE DEAD DOG

JIM DAVIS

7-11

8-8 JIM DAVIS

Find 10 things wrong with this picture.

ANSWERS: 1. Garfield is taking a bath. 2. Arlene is eating Garfield's food. 3. Odie is chasing mice. 4. Pan of lasagna uneaten. 5. Garfield isn't tripping Jon carrying the groceries.

JIM DAVIS

It may have been destined from the very beginning that Jim Davis would create Garfield. Jim grew up on a small farm in Fairmount, Indiana, surrounded by 25 cats. He was asthmatic as a child and was stuck indoors with his paper, pencil, and imagination to play with. It was the imagination that did it.

Jim attended Ball State University as an art and business major and received such honors as one of the lowest cumulative grade point ratios in the history of the university.

After college, Jim went to work for an advertising agency, during which time he met his wife Carolyn, a gifted alto with the Ball State University Singers. (It's been rumored that she tried to teach Jim to sing but gave up in defeat.)

In 1969, Jim started working with Tom Ryan on the syndicated comic strip "Tumbleweeds." Jim's first attempt at his own strip was "Gnorm the Gnat." Gnorm, however, went down in defeat. The syndicates felt it might be a little difficult for readers to relate to a bug.

After months of waiting for that all-important decision, Garfield was accepted in January of 1978 by United Feature Syndicate.

Paws, Inc., an art facility for all Garfield merchandising, is the only studio in existence for a licensed character. The Paws staff grew from three people to fifteen in one year's time.

The Garfield strip is now in over 1,400 papers, making it the fastest growing strip in history. Merchandising for Garfield is worldwide.

With all his success, Jim's favorite things in life are still simple—good friends and good food.